Mc
Graw
Hill
Education

Cover and Title Page: Nathan Love

www.mheonline.com/readingwonders

Send all inquiries to:
McGraw-Hill Education
2 Penn Plaza
New York, NY 10121

ISBN: 978-0-02-131094-4
MHID: 0-02-131094-7

Printed in the United States of America

2 3 4 5 6 7 8 9 RMN 20 19 18 17 16

B

ELD
Companion Worktext

Program Authors

Diane August

Jana Echevarria

Josefina V. Tinajero

Mc
Graw
Hill
Education

Unit 1

Friends and Family

The Big Idea

Friends and Family

The Big Idea

How do families and friends learn, grow, and help one another?

TALK ABOUT IT

Weekly Concept Friends Help Friends

? Essential Question
How do friends depend on each other?

» *Go Digital*

COLLABORATE

What are the friends looking at? How can they help each other? Talk about times friends depend on each other. Write your ideas on the chart.

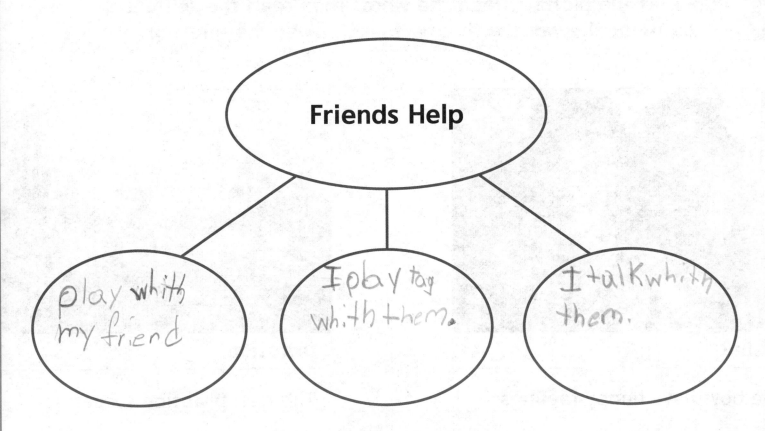

Friends Help

play whith my friend

I play tag whith them.

I talk whith them.

Talk about how friends depend on each other. Use the words from the chart. You can say:

Friends help when _you need it._

Friends can _help you._

5

More Vocabulary

Look at the picture. Read the word. Then read the sentence. Talk about the word with a partner. Answer the questions.

feelings

The boys have happy **feelings**.

What word tells about a *feeling*?

boy   (glad)   gift

What gives you happy feelings?

I have happy feelings when I

when im whith a frend,

practice

The girls **practice** soccer.

Why do we *practice*?

to win   to get better

What do you practice?

I practice _for a math test_
and to get a good grade.

(l)Jill Braaten/McGraw-Hill Education; (r)Erik Isakson/Blend Images/Getty Images

6

Words and Phrases: Homophones *your, you're*

The word *your* tells that something belongs to you.

The pen belongs to you.

It is **your** pen.

The word *you're* is a short way to write *you are*.

You are the winner!

You're the winner!

COLLABORATE

Talk with a partner. Look at the picture. Read the sentence. Write the word that completes the sentence.

Meet __you're__ new friend.

your   (**you're**)

__your_____ a great artist.

(**Your**)   **You're**

COLLABORATE

1 Talk About It

Look at the picture. Read the title. Talk about what you see. Use these words.

birds   nest   little   fly

Who is the story about?

The story is about three

_____.

Where is Little Flap?

He is in his _____.

What does Little Flap learn to do?

Little Flap learns how_____

_____.

Take notes as you read the text.

Little Flap Learns to Fly

Essential Question

? How do friends depend on each other?

Read how Little Flap depends on his friends.

8

Little Flap liked his nest. Fluff and Tuff lived in the **next** nest. Their parents gave them worms to eat.

One day Fluff said, "Let's get our own worms."

Tuff said, "First, we must learn to fly."

Fluff said, "Let's learn!"

Tim Beaumont

❶ **Sentence Structure** Ⓐ Ⓒ Ⓣ

Reread the first sentence. Circle the words that tell who the sentence is about.

❷ **Specific Vocabulary** Ⓐ Ⓒ Ⓣ

The word *next* tells that something is near. Who lives in the next nest, or near Little Flap's nest?

_____

_____ in the next nest.

❸ **Comprehension**
Key Details

Reread the second and third paragraphs. Underline what Fluff wants to get. What must the birds do first?

First, the birds must learn

_____.

9

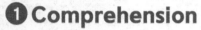

❶ Comprehension

Key Details

Reread the first paragraph. Little Flap looks down from his nest. How does Little Flap feel?

Little Flap feels

_____.

❷ Sentence Structure ⒶⒸⓉ

Reread the last paragraph. What words tell you Fluff speaks to her friends? Circle the words. Underline what Fluff wants to practice with her friends.

❸ Specific Vocabulary ⒶⒸⓉ

Circle the sentence that tells the meaning of the word *flapping*.

Little Flap looked down. His nest was high up. The ground was far away. He felt scared! Little Flap did not tell his friends. He kept his **feelings** a secret.

Fluff said, "Let's **practice flapping** our wings. It will make them strong." Fluff moved her wings up and down.

10

Soon it was time to fly. Little Flap told his friends how he felt. He said, "I'm scared!"

"We are friends," Tuff said. "You can depend on us."

"We will go first," Fluff said. "Then you can try. We will help."

Tuff and Fluff jumped. They flew! "Now it's your turn," Tuff said.

Little Flap watched. He began to feel brave. He said, "I will try."

Tim Beaumont

Text Evidence

COLLABORATE

❶ Talk About It

Reread the second and third paragraphs. Talk about how Little Flap can depend on his friends.

Who will fly first?

_____

Then who can try to fly?

Then _____

_____ to fly.

❷ Comprehension
Key Details

Reread the rest of the page. Little Flap watches his friends. Underline what they do. Circle how this makes Little Flap feel.

11

Text Evidence

1 Sentence Structure ⒶⒸⓉ

The first sentence is about Little Flap. Circle the word that connects two things he does. Underline the two things Little Flap does.

2 Comprehension
Key Details

In the first paragraph, circle what Little Flap can do now.

COLLABORATE

3 Talk About It

Draw boxes around what Fluff and Tuff tell Little Flap. Talk about why they say these things.

Little Flap flapped his wings and counted, "one, two, three!" He jumped. He flew!

"You're flying well!" Fluff said.

Tuff said, "Good for you!"

12

The birds landed on soft grass. Little Flap got a worm. He shared the worm with his friends.

Little Flap was happy. He knew he could **always** depend on Fluff and Tuff.

"Thank you!" Little Flap said.

Now Little Flap likes flying!

Make Connections

? Tell how Little Flap depends on his friends. ESSENTIAL QUESTION

Tell about a time when you depended on your friends.

TEXT TO SELF

Tim Beaumont

1 Comprehension
Key Details

Reread the first paragraph. Underline what Little Flap shares with his friends.

2 Specific Vocabulary Ⓐ©Ⓣ

Reread the second paragraph. The word *always* means "all the time." What does Little Flap know?

Little Flap knows he can

_____

_____.

COLLABORATE

3 Talk About It

How does Little Flap feel about flying now?

Little Flap _____

_____.

13

Respond to the Text

Why does Little Flap feel scared?

Text Evidence 🔍

Little Flap wants to learn to _____. Page(s): _____

But he feels scared when _____. Page(s): _____

At first, Little Flap keeps _____. Page(s): _____

How do Little Flap's friends help?

Text Evidence 🔍

The friends practice _____. Page(s): _____

Fluff and Tuff will go _____. Then Little Flap _____. Page(s): _____

Fluff and Tuff tell Little Flap _____. Page(s): _____

Group Discussion Present your answers to the class. Cite text evidence for your ideas. Listen to and discuss the group's opinions about your ideas.

Write Work with a partner. Look at your notes. Write your answer to the question. Use text evidence to support your answer. Use vocabulary words in your writing.

How does Little Flap depend on his friends?

Little Flap is _____ but does not tell about his

_____. The little birds _____ flapping their

wings. Fluff and Tuff will go _____.

Then LIttle Flap _____ to fly. In the end, Fluff

and Tuff help _____

_____.

Share Writing Present your writing to the class. Discuss their opinions. Talk about their ideas. Explain why you agree or disagree. You can say:

I agree with _____.

I do not agree, because _____.

Write to Sources

pages 8–13

Take Notes About the Text I took notes on this chart to respond to the prompt: *Add to the story. Tell how Little Flap shares a worm with Fluff and Tuff.*

Anita

Little Flap, Fluff, and Tuff want to get worms.

Fluff and Tuff help Little Flap to fly.

Little Flap flies and finds a worm.

Little Flap can help his friends now.

Design Pics/Kristy-Anne Glubish

Write About the Text **My story tells how Little Flap shares a worm.**

Little Flap looked on the ground. He found a big worm. His friends loved worms. Little Flap wanted to do something nice for Fluff and Tuff. Little Flap cut the worm into three pieces. The three friends shared the worm for lunch.

TALK ABOUT IT

Text Evidence **Draw boxes** around the characters that come from the notes. Who did Anita write about?

Grammar **Underline** the word that tells how many. Why did Anita use a number word?

Connect Ideas **Circle** the sentences that tell how Little Flap finds the worm. How can you use *and* to connect the sentences?

Your Turn

Add to the story. Write how Little Flap teaches another bird to fly.

>> *Go Digital*
Write your response online. Use your editing checklist.

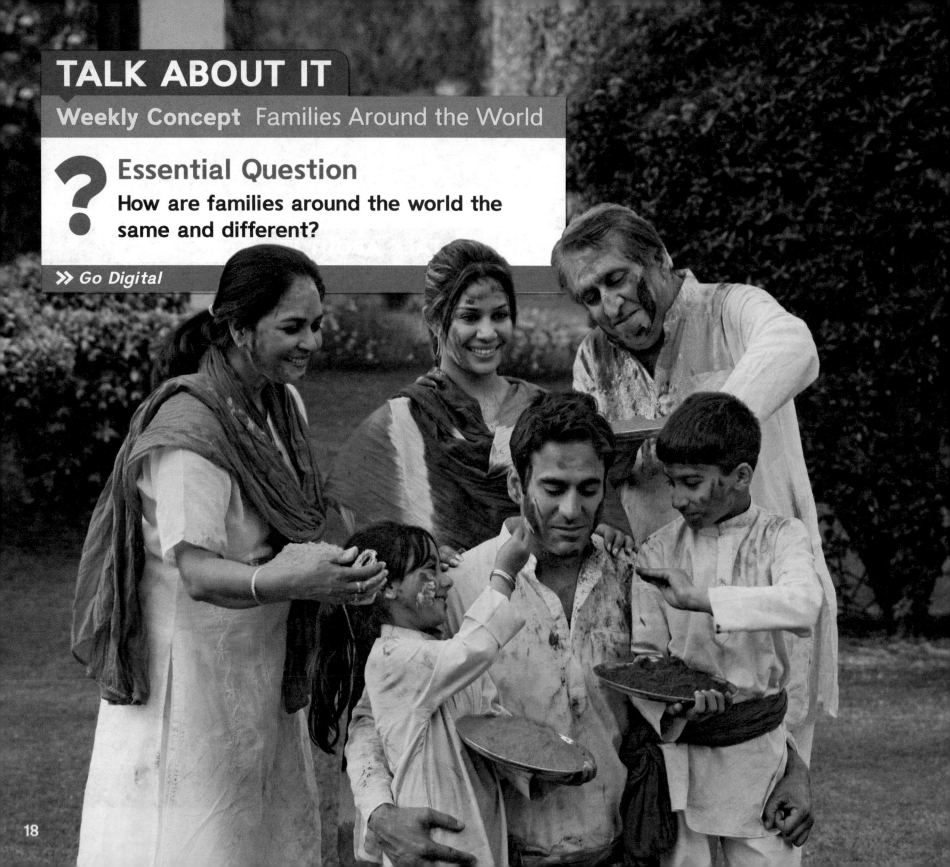

TALK ABOUT IT

Weekly Concept Families Around the World

? Essential Question

How are families around the world the same and different?

>> *Go Digital*

COLLABORATE How does the family celebrate the spring season? How does your family celebrate together? Write how families celebrate in the same ways and in different ways.

Same	Different

Talk about how families celebrate special times. Tell how they can be the same or different. Use the words from the chart. Complete the sentences.

Families around the world _____

_____. Families have different

_____. My family celebrates

_____.

More Vocabulary

COLLABORATE Look at the picture. Read the word. Then read the sentence. Talk about the word with a partner. Answer the questions.

chance

Dan has a **chance** to share ideas.

What is a *chance*?

paper   think   time

When do you have a chance to share ideas?

I have a chance to share ideas

with _____.

proud

Dad is **proud** of me.

What does *proud* mean?

pleased   unhappy   far from

What makes you feel proud?

I feel proud when I _____

_____.

Words and Phrases: Contractions *it's, I'll*

The word *it's* is a short way to write *it is*.

Is it raining today?

It's raining today.

The word *I'll* is a short way to write *I will*.

Will you catch the ball?

I'll catch the ball.

COLLABORATE

Talk with a partner. Look at the pictures. Read the sentences. Write the two words for each underlined word.

Now <u>it's</u> time for lunch.

_____

<u>I'll</u> walk home with you.

_____

(tl)Monica Murphy/Getty Images; (tr)Mark Tooker/iStock/360/Getty Images; (bl)Jose Luis Pelaez Inc/Blend Images LLC; (br)Ariel Skelley/Blend Images LLC

COLLABORATE

1 Talk About It

Look at the picture. Read the title. Talk about what you see. Use these words.

costume   dances   country

Write about what you see.

What does Maria wear?

Maria wears a

_____.

Does Maria dance?

Yes, Maria _____.

What does she celebrate?

Maria celebrates _____

_____ called Brazil.

Take notes as you read the text.

Maria Celebrates Brazil

Essential Question

? **How are families around the world the same and different?**

Read about a family from Brazil.

22

Maria and her family are in their kitchen. "Please!" Maria begs. Maria does not want to go to practice **today**.

Mãe speaks Portuguese. It is the language of Brazil. Mãe says, "You must practice. The parade is **next week**."

Janet Broxon

1 **Sentence Structure** Ⓐ Ⓒ Ⓣ

Who is the first sentence about? Circle the subject. Box the part of the sentence that tells about the people.

2 **Comprehension**
Character, Setting, Events

Reread the second paragraph. Mãe speaks Portuguese. Where does Maria's family come from?

_____

3 **Specific Vocabulary** Ⓐ Ⓒ Ⓣ

The words *next week* and *today* tell order. Complete the sentence with "next week" and "today."

Maria must go to practice

_____ because the

parade is _____.

Text Evidence

1 Sentence Structure ACT

Reread the third paragraph. The pronoun *her* tells who the house belongs to. Circle the name of the person who invited Maria to "her house."

2 Specific Vocabulary ACT

Reread the fourth paragraph. The words *all over* mean "many different places." Why is the parade important?

People from _____

_____ to see it.

3 Comprehension
Character, Setting, Events

The family shares their culture at the parade. Underline details about culture at the parade.

"It's not fair," says Maria.

Mãe says, "Maria, you must do the right thing."

"But Ana invited me to her house," Maria says.

"The parade is important," says Pai. "People from **all over** come to see it. They try our food. They see how we dress. They see how we live. It is a **chance** to share our culture."

Maria says, "But I want to see Ana."

"You can see Ana any time," says Pai. "They are giving out costumes at practice today."

Maria thinks about her father's words. She and her friends have worked hard. They practiced their dance steps. They made colorful costumes.

Janet Broxon

Text Evidence

❶ Comprehension

Character, Setting, Events

Reread what Pai says to Maria. Underline what happens at practice today.

COLLABORATE

❷ Talk About It

Explain what Maria and her friends did for the parade.

Maria and her friends have

_____.

They practiced their _____

_____.

They made _____

_____.

25

1 Comprehension

Character, Setting, Events

Reread the first paragraph. Box what Maria decides to do. Underline why she wants to do this?

2 Sentence Structure Ⓐ Ⓒ Ⓣ

Reread the first sentence in the second paragraph. Circle the phrase that tells when parade day takes place. Box what happens.

COLLABORATE

3 Talk About It

Maria and her group worked hard. What can they do at the parade?

Maria says, "I'll go to practice. I want to dance my best at the parade."

One week later, people line the streets on parade day. Maria's group knows each dance. They move to the beat.

The **crowd** cheers. A lot of people came to watch the parade.

A woman points a camera, so Maria smiles. Click! The woman takes a picture. Maria is **proud** of her hard work!

Janet Broxon

Make Connections

? How does Maria celebrate the culture of her family? ESSENTIAL QUESTION

What does your family celebrate? What are some things that you do? TEXT TO SELF

❶ Specific Vocabulary Ⓐ Ⓒ Ⓣ

Reread the first paragraph. Circle words that help you understand the meaning of *crowd*. Underline two things the crowd does.

❷ Sentence Structure Ⓐ Ⓒ Ⓣ

Reread the first sentence in the second paragraph. The word *so* connects two parts of the sentence. Underline the part that tells why Maria smiles.

COLLABORATE

❸ Talk About It

How does Maria feel about being in the parade?

Maria is _____

_____.

27

Respond to the Text

Partner Discussion Read the questions. Find and show text evidence. Discuss what you learned. Write the page numbers.

Why is the parade important?	Text Evidence 🔍
Mãe says Maria must _____.	Page(s): _____
Pai tells her that the parade is _____.	Page(s): _____
Maria and the other children have _____.	Page(s): _____

What happens at the parade?	Text Evidence 🔍
People line _____.	Page(s): _____
Maria's group moves to _____.	Page(s): _____
Maria is _____ of her hard work.	Page(s): _____

Group Discussion Present your answers to the group. Cite text evidence for your ideas. Listen to and discuss the group's opinions.

Write Work with a partner. Look at your notes. Write your answer to the question. Use text evidence to support your answer. Use vocabulary words in your writing.

How does Maria celebrate the culture of Brazil?

Maria is going to be in a _____.

It is important because it is a _____ for

Maria to _____ her culture. Maria feels

_____ of her hard work.

Share Writing Present your writing to the class. Discuss their opinions. Talk about their ideas. Explain why you agree or disagree. You can say:

I agree with _____.

I do not agree, because _____.

Write to Sources

Alex

pages 22–27

Take Notes About the Text I took notes about the text on the web to respond to the prompt: *Write a paragraph. Tell about Maria's costume.*

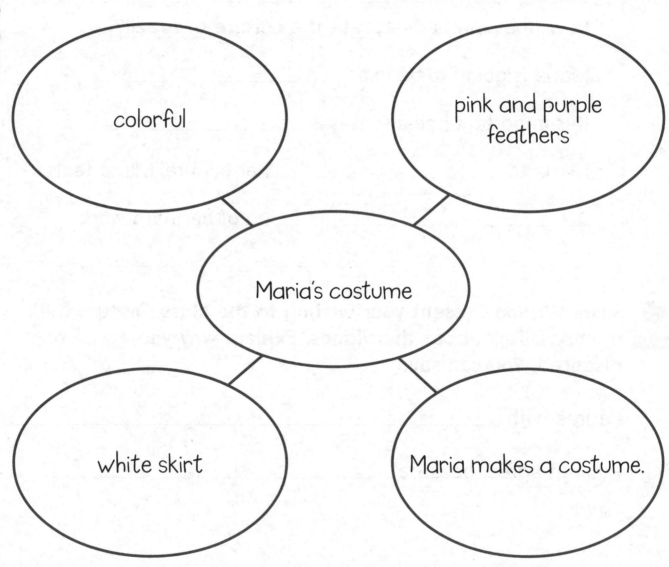

colorful

pink and purple feathers

Maria's costume

white skirt

Maria makes a costume.

Write About the Text **My paragraph describes Maria's costume.**

Maria makes a colorful costume. It has feathers. They are pink and purple. It has a white skirt. Her costume sparkles. It is pretty for the parade!

TALK ABOUT IT

Text Evidence Underline words that tell the colors of Maria's costume. What other words tell what her costume looks like?

Grammar Circle a verb. What verb tense did Alex use to describe what the costume looks like?

Condense Ideas Box the sentences about feathers. How can you condense the ideas into one sentence?

Your Turn

Look at the parade on page 27. Use details from the story to help you write a paragraph about the parade.

>> Go Digital
Write your response online. Use your editing checklist.

31

TALK ABOUT IT

Weekly Concept Pets Are Our Friends

? **Essential Question**
How can a pet be an
important friend?

» *Go Digital*

32

COLLABORATE

What pet do you see in the picture? How is the pet a friend? Write on the chart ways pets can be important friends.

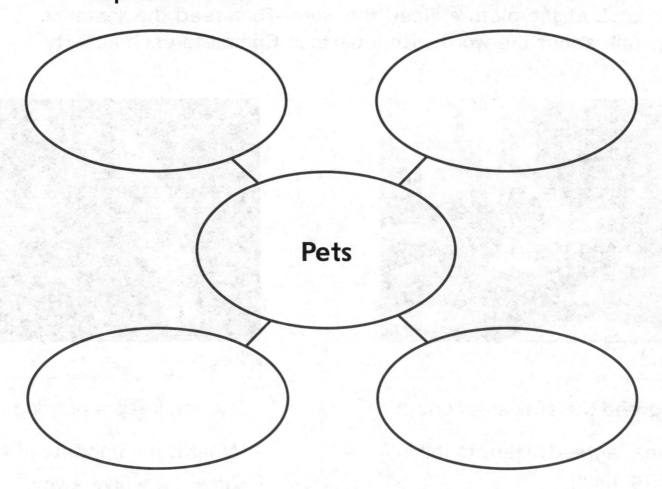

Pets

Talk about how pets can be our friends. Use the words from the chart. You can say:

_____ can be our friends because they _____.

Pets _____ us.

More Vocabulary

Look at the picture. Read the word. Then read the sentence. Talk about the word with a partner. Complete each activity.

agreed

We **agreed** the answer is correct.

The word *agreed* means to think the same thing.

What did your class agree about?

My class agreed _____

_____.

keep

She can **keep** a pet dog.

What is the opposite of *keep*?
show   give away   find

Name pets people keep.

People keep pet _____

or _____.

Words and Phrases: Homophones *dogs, dog's*

The word *dogs* means "more than one dog."

I see more than one dog.

I see two **dogs**.

The word *dog's* tells when something belongs to a dog.

The dog has brown fur.

The **dog's** fur is brown.

Talk with a partner. Look at the picture. Read the sentence. Write the word that completes the sentence.

The _____ play.

dogs   dog's

The _____ bowl is empty.

dogs   dog's

35

COLLABORATE

1 Talk About It

Look at the pictures. Read the title. Talk about what you see. Use these words.

dog   pet   petting

Write about what you see.

The story is about a boy

named Jake who _____

_____

named _____ .

What is Jake doing?

Jake is _____

the dog.

Take notes as you read the text.

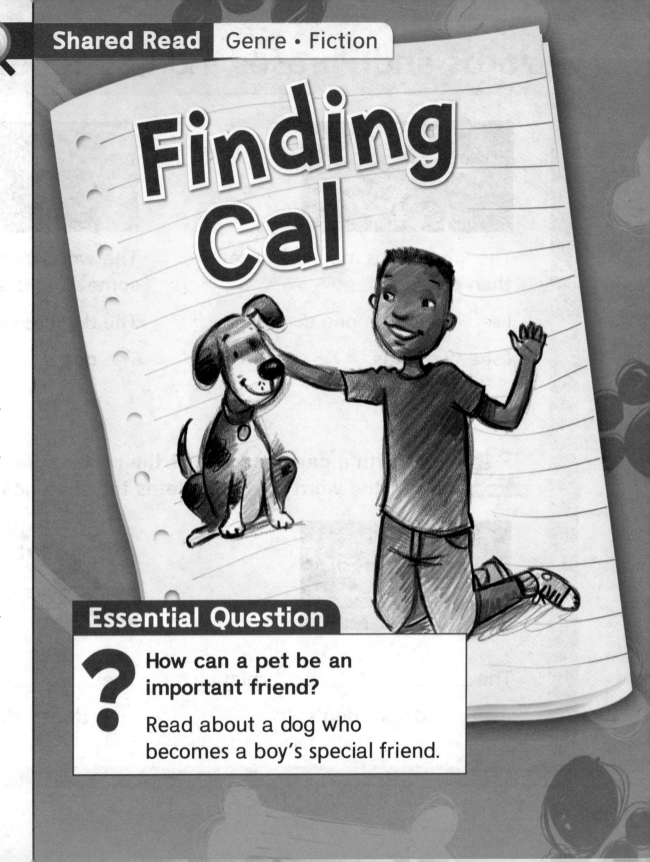

Finding Cal

Essential Question

? How can a pet be an important friend?

Read about a dog who becomes a boy's special friend.

September 25

Dear Diary,

Dad said yes! He said I can get a dog! But the dog must not be large. The dog's size must be **small or medium**. We will visit, or go to, the animal shelter tomorrow.

Medium Dog

Small Dog

Marcin Piwowarski

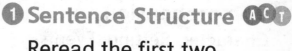

Text Evidence

1 Sentence Structure (A)(C)(T)

Reread the first two sentences. Find the pronoun *he*. Circle the person that the pronoun *he* refers to.

2 Specific Vocabulary (A)(C)(T)

Reread the next two sentences. The words *small or medium* tell the sizes the dog must be. Underline the word that tells the size the dog must *not* be.

3 Comprehension
Character, Setting, Events

What will the boy and Dad do tomorrow?

The boy and his dad will

_____

_____

_____ .

Text Evidence 🔍

❶ Comprehension
Character, Setting, Events

Reread the first paragraph. What does Jake see at the shelter? Underline the sentence that tells you.

❷ Specific Vocabulary 🅐🅒🅣

The word *soft* means "not hard or not stiff." What word in the first paragraph has the opposite meaning of *soft*? Box the word.

❸ Sentence Structure 🅐🅒🅣

In the second paragraph, the words *that dog* refer to a dog you already read about. Circle the name of "that dog." What does Jake know about that dog?

Jake knows _____

_____ him.

Dear Diary,

September 26

Wow! Today I saw big and little dogs. Some dogs have **soft** fur. Other dogs have wiry hair.

We walked to one dog's cage. The tag said Cal. I knew that dog was for me. Dad said, "Look, Jake. See how Cal stares at you?" It was true. Cal's eyes were open wide. He was looking right at me.

Jack   Spot   Sam   Cal

We put Cal on a leash. We took him outside of the shelter. Cal smiled at me. He wanted to play. I patted Cal on the head. He licked my hand.

Cal licking my hand!

Marcin Piwowarski

❶ Comprehension

Character, Setting, Events

Reread the second sentence. Circle the words that tell where the characters go.

❷ Sentence Structure Ⓐ Ⓒ Ⓣ

Reread the third sentence. Box the word that tells who the sentence is about. Underline the text that tells what the subject does.

COLLABORATE

❸ Talk About It

Reread the last three sentences. Write about what Jake and Cal do.

Jake _____ Cal on

the head. Cal _____

his hand.

Text Evidence

Comprehension
Character, Setting, Events

Reread the first paragraph. Who make a great pair of friends already?

_____

2 Specific Vocabulary ACT

The word *nervous* means "to feel something bad can happen." Cal is nervous. Underline how Jake wants Cal to feel.

COLLABORATE

3 Talk About It

What is Cal learning?

Cal learns _____
_____.

Now Cal _____

_____

Dad said, "You guys already make a great pair of friends." I **agreed**.

Soon we started home. Cal was **nervous**. I wanted to make him feel safe. I scratched his ears. He liked that.

Dear Diary,   October 10

I was too busy to write. Cal is learning many tricks. Now he can roll over and stand up.

Cal's Tricks!

Every day Cal and Dad walk to school with me. Every night Cal sleeps with me. I will not trade him for any dog. I will **keep** him because we have a great friendship. Finding Cal was **worth the wait**!

zzZZZZ

Make Connections

? How is Cal an important friend to Jake? ESSENTIAL QUESTION

Do you have or know a pet? How is that pet like Cal? Tell how each pet is a friend. TEXT TO SELF

Text Evidence

1 Comprehension
Character, Setting, Events

What does Cal do every day and every night? Underline these details.

2 Sentence Structure A C T

Reread the fourth sentence. The word *because* connects two parts of a sentence. Underline the two parts. Why will Jake keep Cal?

Jake will keep Cal because

they _____

_____.

3 Specific Vocabulary A C T

The words *worth the wait* mean "good enough to wait for." Circle what Jake thinks was worth the wait.

Respond to the Text

Partner Discussion Read the questions. Find and show text evidence. Discuss what you learned. Write the page numbers.

How does Jake find his pet dog, Cal?

Dad says Jake can _____.

Jake sees Cal and knows Cal is _____.

Dad says Cal and Jake make a great _____.

Text Evidence 🔍

Page(s): _____

Page(s): _____

Page(s): _____

How is Cal a good pet for Jake?

Cal learns _____.

Every day Cal and Dad _____.

Every night Cal sleeps _____.

Text Evidence 🔍

Page(s): _____

Page(s): _____

Page(s): _____

Group Discussion Present your answers to the group. Cite text evidence for your ideas. Listen to and discuss the group's opinions about your ideas.

Write Work with a partner. Look at your notes. Write your answer to the question. Use text evidence to support your answer. Use a vocabulary word in your writing.

COLLABORATE

How is Cal an important friend to Jake?

Dad says Jake and Cal make a great _____

_____. Jake _____.

Cal learns _____.

Every day, Dad and Cal _____

_____. Every night, Cal _____

_____. They have a great _____.

Share Writing Present your writing to the class. Discuss their opinions. Talk about their ideas. Explain why you agree or disagree. You can say:

I agree with _____.

I do not agree because _____.

Write to Sources

pages 36–41

James

Take Notes About the Text I took notes about the text on this chart to respond to the prompt: *Add a diary entry. Have Jake teach Cal a trick.*

Jake and Dad find Cal at the animal shelter.

⬇

Cal learns new tricks.

⬇

Cal learns to roll over.

⬇

Cal walks to school with Jake. Cal sleeps with Jake. Cal and Jake are friends.

Write About the Text **My diary entry tells about teaching Cal a new trick.**

Student Model: *Narrative Text*

October 15

Dear Diary,

Cal can roll over. I teach Cal to shake hands. I put out my hand. I say, "Shake." Cal puts his paw in my hand. We shake hands because we are friends.

TALK ABOUT IT

Text Evidence **Circle** one detail that comes from the chart. Why did James use it in his diary entry?

Grammar **Draw a box** around the subject of the first sentence. What does the subject tell?

Connect Ideas **Underline** the third and fourth sentences. How can you use the word *and* to connect the sentences?

Your Turn

Write a diary entry for the beginning of the story. Write about when Jake asks Dad for a dog.

>> Go Digital
Write your response online. Use your editing checklist.

COLLABORATE What animal do you see? How do people care for this animal? Write on the chart ways we care for animals.

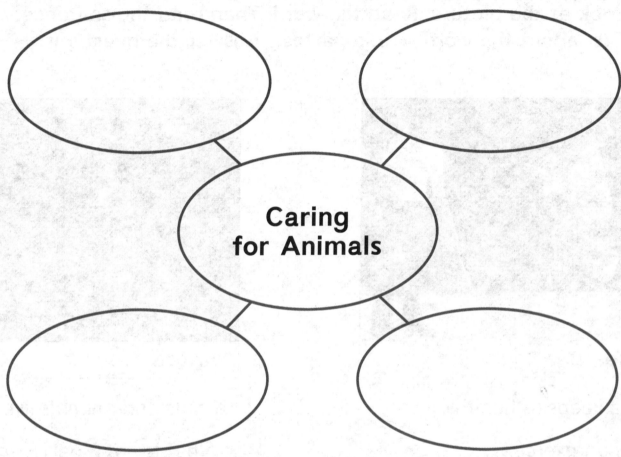

Caring for Animals

Talk about ways people care for animals. Use the words from the chart. You can say:

People give animals _____ .

Animals need a safe place to _____

_____ .

More Vocabulary

**Look at the picture. Read the word. Then read the sentence.
Talk about the word with a partner. Answer the questions.**

exercise

Exercise keeps us healthy.

What is an *exercise*?

running   bringing   telling

What is your favorite exercise?

My favorite exercise is _____

_____.

nature

Plants and animals live in **nature**.

What is *not* a part of *nature*?

trees   schools   squirrels

Why do you like nature?

I like nature because _____

_____.

(l)AGB Photo/Alamy; (r)Design Pics/Michael Interisano

48

Words and Phrases: Homographs *leaves*

The word *leaves* means "more than one leaf."

What falls from the trees?

The **leaves** fall from the trees.

The word *leaves* tells when someone goes away.

What is the girl doing now?

She **leaves** on her bike.

COLLABORATE Talk with a partner. Look at the picture. Read the sentence. Circle the meaning of the word *leaves*.

Joel and Mom rake leaves.

more than one leaf
goes away

Mom leaves for work.

more than one leaf
goes away

COLLABORATE

1 Talk About It

Look at the pictures. Read the title. Talk about what you see. Use these words.

horse   farm   boy

Write about what you see.

The text is about _____

_____

_____

_____.

Where are the boy and the horse?

The boy and the horse are

_____.

Take notes as you read the text.

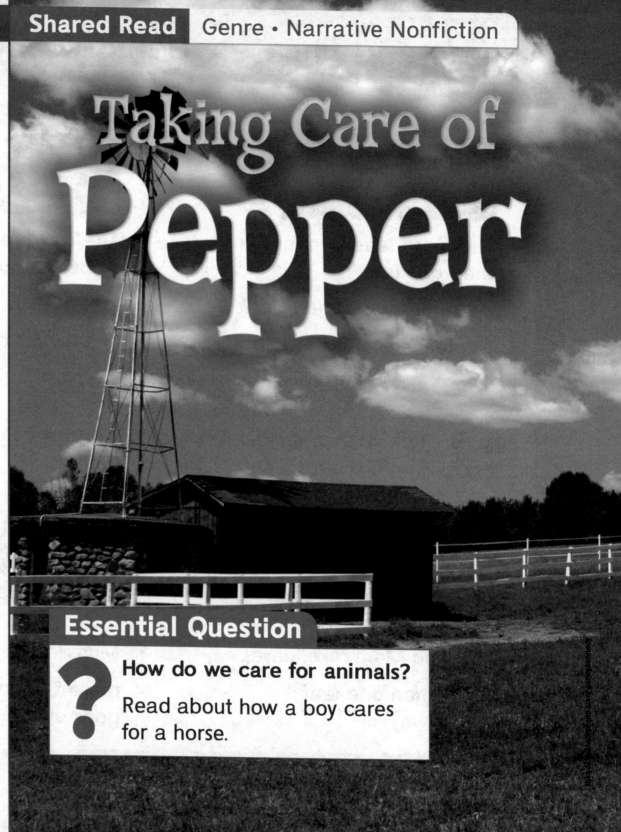

Taking Care of Pepper

Essential Question

? **How do we care for animals?**

Read about how a boy cares for a horse.

Jack lives on a farm. He has a horse named Pepper. Jack helps take care of Pepper. It is a big job. A horse needs many things to live.

1 Sentence Structure (A)(C)(T)

Reread the first two sentences. The pronoun *he* refers to a boy. Circle the name of the boy. Who has a horse named Pepper?

_____

a horse named Pepper.

2 Comprehension

Key Details

Reread the rest of the page. Why is it a big job to take care of Pepper?

A horse _____

_____

_____.

Text Evidence

1 **Specific Vocabulary** ⒶⒸⓉ

Reread the first paragraph. What words tell you the meaning of *stall*? Box the words.

2 **Comprehension**

Key Details

Look back at the caption for the picture. Pepper is happy to see Jack. How does Pepper show this? Underline the words that tell you.

3 **Sentence Structure** ⒶⒸⓉ

Read the last paragraph. Jack is the subject in each sentence. Underline what Jack does in each sentence.

Pepper stomps his hoof and nods his head when he sees Jack.

Every morning, Jack wakes up at 5:00 a.m. Jack and Dad go to Pepper's **stall**. This small room for a horse keeps Pepper safe.

Pepper is happy to see Jack.

First, Jack gives Pepper hay to eat. Then Jack cleans. Jack takes out the dirty hay and sawdust.

Tom Joslyn/Alamy

Next, Jack pets Pepper's brown **coat**. It feels smooth. Then Jack leaves for school. But his work is not done!

At 3:00 p.m., Jack rides the bus back home. He has a snack. He does his homework. Then Jack gets an apple for Pepper. It is time to visit the horse.

Jack feeds Pepper.
Jack gives Pepper water.

Andy Crawford and Kit Houghton/Getty Images

❶ **Specific Vocabulary** Ⓐ Ⓒ Ⓣ

Reread the first two sentences. A *coat* is the hair on a horse's skin. Circle two words that describe Pepper's coat.

❷ **Comprehension**
Key Details

In the first paragraph, underline what Jack does after he pets Pepper.

COLLABORATE

❸ **Talk About It**

Talk about what Jacks does after school. What does Jack do after homework?

Jack gets _____

_____

_____

53

Text Evidence

❶ Specific Vocabulary Ⓐ❶Ⓣ

Reread the third sentence. To *walk around* can mean to walk to many parts of a place. Box where Pepper can walk around.

❷ Comprehension

Key Details

Reread the second paragraph. Underline what horses do in the wild. What does Pepper do each day on the farm?

Jack makes sure Pepper

_____

_____ .

Jack and Mom find Pepper. He is in a field. Pepper can **walk around** the field. Pepper drinks cool water. Walking made him thirsty!

Now it is time for Pepper's **exercise**. Horses run a lot in the wild. But Pepper does not live out in **nature**. Jack makes sure Pepper runs each day.

Pepper must exercise each day.

Carol Walker/naturepl.com

54

Jack puts the saddle on Pepper. Mom does the same with her horse. They ride their horses.

When they finish riding, Jack grooms Pepper. He brushes his mane and tail.

Finally, Jack gives Pepper more hay. He gives him water, too. Jack says, "See you in the morning." Pepper nods his head. It is his way to say, "I'll be waiting!"

Jack's Dad checks for rocks in Pepper's hooves.

Make Connections

? How do people care for horses?
ESSENTIAL QUESTION

Compare the needs of a horse and another pet you know. Which needs more care? TEXT TO SELF

Text Evidence

1 Sentence Structure (A)(C)(T)

Reread the second paragraph. Box the words in the first sentence that tell what happens when they finish riding.

2 Comprehension
Key Details

How does Jack groom Pepper?

Jack _____

his mane and _____.

COLLABORATE

3 Talk About It

Talk about the end of Pepper's day. Underline why Pepper nods his head after Jack says, "See you in the morning."

Respond to the Text

Partner Discussion Read the questions. Find and show text evidence. Discuss what you learned. Write the page numbers.

Why does Jack take care of Pepper?

Pepper lives _____. Pepper does not live _____.

A horse needs many things to _____.

Jack must keep _____ clean.

Text Evidence 🔍

Page(s): _____

Page(s): _____

Page(s): _____

What are some things a horse needs?

A stall keeps _____.

Horses need to eat _____ and drink _____.

Pepper needs to run. Horses need _____.

Text Evidence 🔍

Page(s): _____

Page(s): _____

Page(s): _____

COLLABORATE

Group Discussion Present your answers to the group. Cite text evidence for your ideas. Listen to and discuss the group's opinions.

Write Work with a partner. Look at your notes. Write your answer to the question. Use text evidence to support your answer. Use vocabulary words in your writing.

> **How does Jack care for Pepper?**
>
> Pepper does not live in _____.
>
> Taking care of a horse is a _____. Jack
>
> gives Pepper _____ to eat and _____
>
> to drink. Jack brushes Pepper's _____.
>
> Jack lets Pepper run each day because _____
>
> _____.

Share Writing Present your writing to the class. Discuss their opinions. Talk about their ideas. Explain why you agree or disagree. You can say:

I agree with _____.

I do not agree because _____.

Write to Sources

Sophie

Take Notes About the Text I took notes on the text to answer the question: *Is it easy or hard to take care of a horse? Explain why.*

pages 50–55

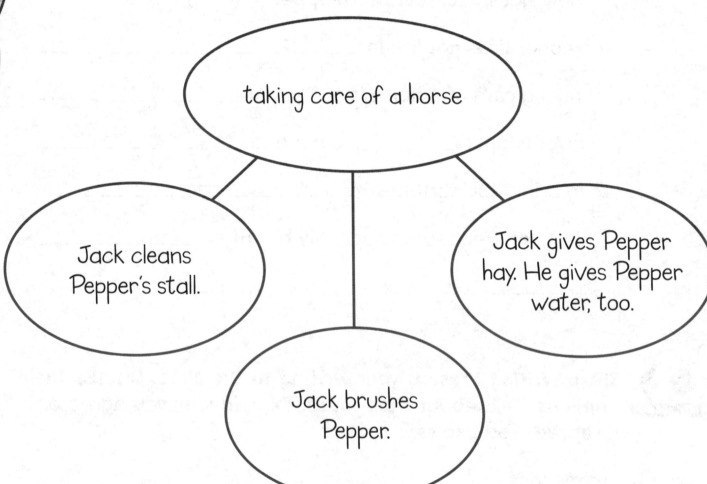

taking care of a horse

Jack cleans Pepper's stall.

Jack gives Pepper hay. He gives Pepper water, too.

Jack brushes Pepper.

Write About the Text **My paragraph tells my opinion about taking care of a horse.**

It is hard to take care of a horse. First, Jack gives Pepper hay. He cleans Pepper's stall. He also needs to brush Pepper. He brushes Pepper's mane and tail. At the end of the day, he feeds Pepper again.

TALK ABOUT IT

COLLABORATE

Text Evidence **Box** what Jack gives Pepper first. What detail from the chart could you add after this sentence?

Grammar **Circle** the phrase *at the end of the day*. What does Jack do at this time?

Condense Ideas **Underline** the fourth and fifth sentences. How can you condense the ideas into one sentence?

Your Turn

COLLABORATE

Could you take care of a horse? Think about what Jack did. Use that in your answer.

>> Go Digital
Write your response online. Use your editing checklist.

? **Essential Question**
What happens when
families work together?

>> *Go Digital*

COLLABORATE

What is the family doing? How do they work together? Talk about times families work together. Write your ideas on the chart.

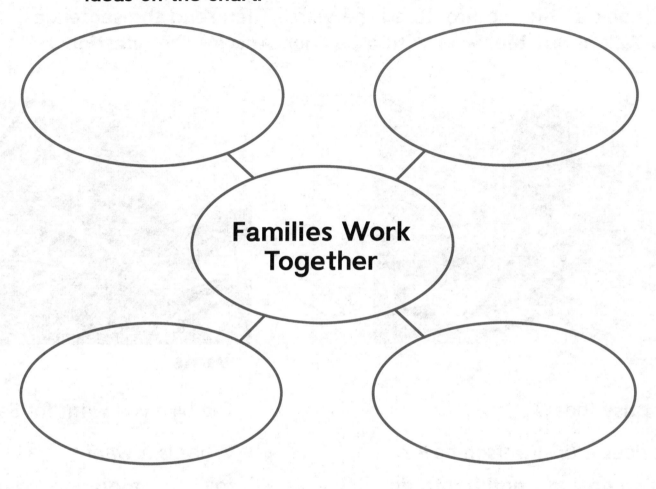

Families Work Together

Talk about ways families work together. Use the words from the chart. You can say:

A family works together to _____.

A family can help _____.

More Vocabulary

Look at the picture. Read the word. Then read the sentence. Talk about the word with a partner. Answer the questions.

busy

She is **busy** today.

What does a *busy* person have?

things to do   **nothing to do**

What makes a day busy?

In a busy day, I _____

_____.

wants

The bike is a **want** for Sam.

What is a *want*?

toy   **food**   **water**

What is one of your wants?

One of my wants is _____

_____.

Words and Phrases: Articles *a, the*

Use *a* to tell about one thing.

I see **a** blue bird.

Use *the* to tell about more than one thing.

The birds fly away.

COLLABORATE

Talk with a partner. Look at the picture. Read the sentence. Write the word that completes the sentence.

It is _____ white boat.

    a   the

_____ boats are pretty.

    A   The

COLLABORATE

1 Talk About It

Look at the photographs. Read the title. Talk about what you see. Use these words.

doctor firefighter family

Write about what you see.

The text is about _____

_____

_____.

Who are the people?

The people are _____

_____

_____.

Take notes as you read the text.

Essential Question

?

What happens when families work together?

Read about how one family works to meet their needs.

Families Work!

Ellen Yung had a **busy** day. She helped twenty kids! Ellen is a doctor for children. She works many hours. Doctors have hard jobs.

Steve is Ellen's husband. He is a **firefighter**. He works hard. Steve checks the fire trucks and hoses. The firefighters work together to put out fires.

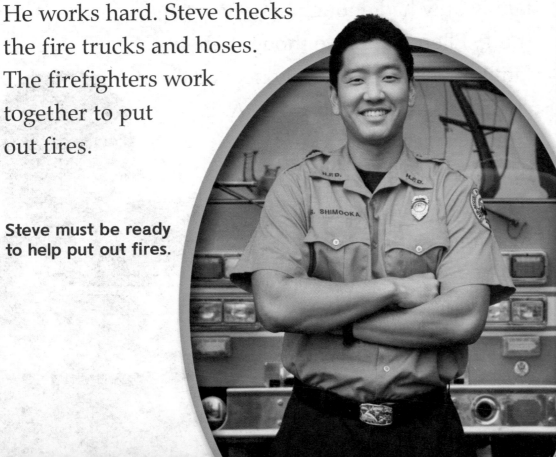

Steve must be ready to help put out fires.

1 Sentence Structure AT

Reread the first paragraph. The pronoun *she* refers to a person. Circle the person in the first sentence.

2 Comprehension

Key Details

Underline why Ellen had a busy day. Draw a box around Ellen's job. Why is the job hard?

She _____

_____.

3 Specific Vocabulary AT

Reread the second paragraph. Why do *firefighters* work together? Box the text that tells you.

❶ Comprehension

Key Details

Reread the first paragraph. The family works together. Underline the work Mom and Hanna do. Circle the work Dad and Zac do.

❷ Specific Vocabulary Ⓐ Ⓒ Ⓣ

Reread the last paragraph. People use a *washing machine* to wash clothes. Underline why the family needed a washing machine.

COLLABORATE

❸ Talk About It

Underline what the family bought. Why did the family not buy a laptop?

Zac did not _____

_____.

The Yung family works together too. Mom and Hanna dust and mop. Dad and Zac do the laundry. Mom makes a shopping list. She lists items they need and want.

One day, Zac wanted a new laptop. The family needed a new **washing machine**. Both items cost the same. The family only had enough money for one thing. Ellen and Steve thought about the family's needs. The family needed clean clothes for school and work. A laptop is nice. But Zac did not need it. The family bought the washing machine.

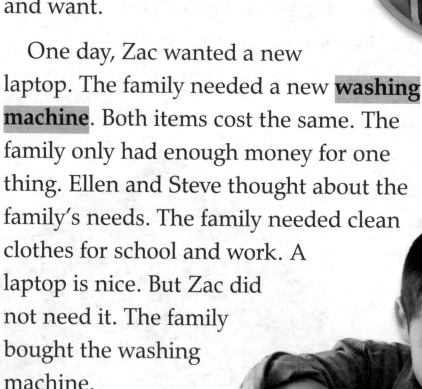

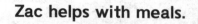

Zac helps with meals.

(t) hana/Datacraft/imagenavi/Getty Images; (b) MIXA next/Getty Images

What Are Some Needs and Wants?

Needs	Wants
Water	Skateboard
Food	Video game
Shelter	Basketball
Clothing	

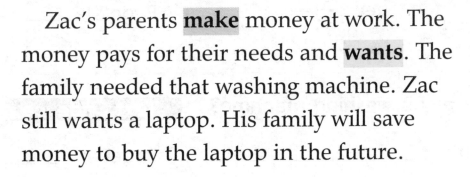

Zac's parents **make** money at work. The money pays for their needs and **wants**. The family needed that washing machine. Zac still wants a laptop. His family will save money to buy the laptop in the future.

Make Connections

? How does the Yung family work together? ESSENTIAL QUESTION

How is your family alike or different from the family in the story? TEXT TO SELF

Text Evidence

1 Specific Vocabulary ACT

Reread the first sentence. The word *make* can mean "to earn, or to get." Circle where Zac's parents make money.

2 Sentence Structure ACT

Reread the second sentence. Underline the word that connects the two things the money pays for. Box the two things.

3 Comprehension
Key Details

How will Zac's family buy a laptop?

Zac's family will _____

_____

_____ in the future.

Respond to the Text

Partner Discussion **Read the questions. Find and show text evidence. Discuss what you learned. Write the page numbers.**

What kind of work does the Yung family do?

Ellen Yung helps children. She is a _____.

Steve is a firefighter. He _____.

The family works _____ too. They _____.

Text Evidence 🔍

Page(s): _____

Page(s): _____

Page(s): _____

Why does the Yung family buy a washing machine?

The family had only enough _____.

They thought about their family's _____.

The family needed the washing machine for _____.

Text Evidence 🔍

Page(s): _____

Page(s): _____

Page(s): _____

Group Discussion **Present your answers to the group. Cite text evidence for your ideas. Listen to and discuss the group's opinions.**

Write Work with a partner. Look at your notes. Write your answer to the question. Use text evidence to support your answer. Use vocabulary words in your writing.

COLLABORATE

> **How does the Yung family work together?**
>
> Hanna and Mom _____ at home.
>
> Zac and Dad _____.
>
> Mom and Dad make money at their busy _____.
>
> The money pays for their _____ and _____.
>
> They bought a _____ they need. They will
>
> _____ money to buy _____ Zac wants.

Share Writing Present your writing to the class. Discuss their opinions. Talk about their ideas. Explain why you agree or disagree. You can say:

COLLABORATE

I agree with _____.

I disagree because _____.

Write to Sources

pages 64–67

Lee

Take Notes About the Text I took notes about the text and the "Wants and Needs" chart. I used my notes to answer the question: *What does the chart tell about what families need?*

Families need water.

Families need food.

Families get what they need first.

Families need shelter.

Families need clothing.

Write About the Text **I wrote about what families need.**

Families use money to buy the things that they need. The chart tells four things families need. They need water. They need food. They need shelter and clothing.

TALK ABOUT IT

Text Evidence **Draw boxes** around details that name what families need. Why did Lee put these in his paragraph?

Grammar **Circle** the predicate in the second sentence. What verb could you use instead of *tells?*

Condense Ideas **Underline** the sentences that tell about what families drink and eat. How can you use *and* to connect the needs into one sentence?

Your Turn

What does the family in the story need? Why do they need it? Use details from the text in your answer.

>> Go Digital
Write your response online. Use your editing checklist.

71